CHINA: the New Super power?

Rise of China: As SuperPower

Uzair Ansari & Marjina Sultana

TABLE OF CONTENTS

D. Ecological Issues

E. Reactions and Criticism

F. Accusations of Neo-imperialism and debt trap diplomacy

VII. Cultural and Ideological differences.   **[50]**

IX.The Role of the Private Sector   **[51]**

X.Analysis and Conclusion.   **[52 -53]**

A. Factors contributing to China's rise

B. The impact of the rise of China on the world

C. The future of China's role in the world

This outline provides a general structure for the book, and you can add more detail and depth to each section as you see fit. Additionally, consider including primary source materials, such as government documents, newspaper articles, and personal accounts, to support your arguments and bring historical events to life for readers.

Preface

In recent decades, the world has witnessed the rise of a new global superpower – China. The transformation of this ancient nation into a major economic, political and military power has been nothing short of remarkable. In this book, we delve into the reasons behind this rise and its implications for the world.

China's rise has been characterised by rapid economic growth, military expansion, and a growing assertiveness in international affairs. Its impact on the global order has been significant and is only expected to grow in the coming years. The country's size, population, and economic strength make it a formidable player in the global arena.

In this book, we examine the factors that have driven China's rise and its impact on the world. We explore its economic, political, and military power, and its place in the international community. We also examine the challenges that China faces, including economic, political and social issues, and how they are being addressed by the government and its people.

The rise of China as a superpower has major implications for the world. It is reshaping the global balance of power, creating new opportunities and challenges, and changing the way in which we think about international relations. Whether it will continue on its current path, and what the future holds for China and the world, remains to be seen.

This book provides a comprehensive and insightful examination of the rise of China as a superpower and its impact on the world. It is aimed at students, scholars, policymakers, and anyone interested in understanding the current global landscape and the role that China plays in it.

I. INTRODUCTION

The rise of China in modern times is a story of incredible transformation and growth. For centuries, China was one of the world's leading civilizations, renowned for its art, culture, and technological advancements. However, by the 19th century, China was in a state of decline, plagued by internal strife and foreign domination.

In this book, we will explore the history of China's rise in modern times, which encompasses the late Qing Dynasty (1840-1912), the Republic of China (1912-1949), and the People's Republic of China (1949-present). During this period, China underwent profound changes, moving from an imperial dynasty to a republic, and then to a communist state, before emerging as a major global power in the 21st century.

The term "modern times" refers to the period following the Industrial Revolution, which took place in Europe and North America in the 18th and 19th centuries. This period was characterized by significant advances in science and technology, as well as increased global interconnectedness.

The purpose of this book is to examine the factors that have contributed to China's rise in modern times and to provide a comprehensive overview of this period in Chinese history. We will explore the events and individuals that have shaped China's journey, as well as the challenges and obstacles that the country has faced along the way.

By studying the history of China's rise in modern times, we can gain a deeper understanding of the country's past, present, and future, and the role that it will play in shaping the world in the coming decades.

A. Brief history of China prior to the 20th century

The earliest known written records of China's history date back to 1250 BC from the Shang dynasty, during the reign of King Wu Ding. Ancient historical texts, such as the Book of Documents, the Bamboo Annals and the Records of the Grand Historian, describe a Xia dynasty before the Shang, but no writing from this period has been found, and there is no mention of it in Shang writings. The Yellow River valley, where the Shang ruled, is considered the birthplace of Chinese civilization, although other civilizations developed along the Yellow River and Yangtze River prior to the Shang. China is one of the world's oldest civilizations, with a continuous history of thousands of years.

The Zhou dynasty replaced the Shang and introduced the concept of the Mandate of Heaven to justify their rule. The Zhou government weakened in the 8th century BC, and the country eventually split into smaller states during the Spring and Autumn period. These states became independent and fought against each other during the Warring States period. It was during this time that traditional Chinese culture, literature and philosophy developed. The rival kingdoms developed bureaucratic systems that allowed them to control vast territories directly, which laid the foundation for the imperial system of government.

In 221 BC, Qin Shi Huang conquered the warring states and proclaimed himself the emperor of the Qin dynasty, marking the beginning of imperial China. However, the government soon fell after his death and was replaced by the Han dynasty. The scholar-officials handled administrative tasks during the 21 centuries from 206 BC to 1912. Young men who were knowledgeable in calligraphy, history, literature, and philosophy were selected through difficult government exams. The last dynasty was the Qing dynasty, which was replaced by the Republic of China in 1912 and then the People's Republic of China in 1949. The People's Republic of China and the Republic of China both claim to be the sole legitimate government of China, which has led to a continued dispute. Hong Kong and Macau became special administrative regions of the People's Republic of China after transferring sovereignty from the United Kingdom and Portugal in 1997 and 1999 respectively.

China's history has alternated between periods of political unity and peace and periods of war and failed statehood. At times, the region was dominated by steppe peoples, such as the Mongols and Manchus, many of whom were assimilated into Han Chinese culture and population. Chinese dynasties have ruled parts or all of China at various times, with control stretching as far as Xinjiang, Tibet and Inner Mongolia. The modern culture of China is influenced by traditional culture, other parts of Asia, and the Western world, carried by immigration, cultural assimilation, expansion and foreign contact.

. Explanation of the term "modern times"

"Modern times" in the context of China's history typically refers to the period from the late 19th century to the present day. This period is characterised by rapid and far-reaching changes, as China struggled to adapt to the challenges of modernization and the growing influence of the West.

During this time, China experienced a series of political, social, and economic upheavals, including the decline of the Qing dynasty, the rise of nationalism, the formation of the Republic of China, the Chinese Civil War, the establishment of the People's Republic of China, and the country's ongoing modernization effort.

"Modern times" can also refer to a broader historical period, encompassing the shift from feudal and agrarian societies to more complex, industrialized, and globally connected societies. In this sense, "modern times" in China's history reflect the country's transformation from an isolated, inward-looking imperial state to a dynamic and influential player on the global stage.

C. Overview of the purpose and Scope of the book

The purpose of this book is to provide an in-depth analysis of the rise of China in modern times, exploring the key events, people, and forces that have shaped the country's journey from a declining imperial power to a global economic and political powerhouse.

The book will begin by providing a brief overview of China's history prior to the 20th century including the late Qing Dynasty and the growing pressure from foreign powers. This will be followed by a detailed examination of the key events and developments that have shaped China's rise, including the fall of the Qing dynasty, the rise of nationalism, the formation of the Republic of China, the Chinese Civil War, the establishment of the People's Republic of China, and the country's ongoing modernization effort.

In addition to exploring the political and economic forces that have shaped China's rise, the book will also examine the cultural and social factors that have contributed to this process, including the influence of Confucianism, the role of education, and the impact of globalisation.

The scope of the book will encompass a wide range of topics and perspectives, drawing on a range of sources, including historical documents, government reports, academic studies, and personal accounts, to provide a comprehensive and nuanced understanding of China's rise.

In conclusion, this book aims to provide a comprehensive and engaging examination of the rise of China in modern times, exploring the complex and interrelated factors that have shaped this process and illuminating the country's ongoing transformation and its implications for the world.

II. THE LATE QING DYNASTY (1840-1912)

The late Qing Dynasty was a time of great turmoil and change in China. In the mid-19th century, the country was rocked by a series of foreign invasions, including the First Opium War (1839-1842) and the Second Opium War (1856-1860). These wars resulted in the defeat of the Qing government and the imposition of unequal treaties on China by the victorious Western powers.

The Opium Wars had a profound impact on China, as they demonstrated the country's military weakness and technological backwardness relative to the West. The wars also resulted in the widespread addiction of Chinese citizens to opium, a drug that was introduced to the country by Western merchants.

In addition to the Opium Wars, the late Qing Dynasty was also marked by the Taiping Rebellion (1851-1864), a massive uprising against the government led by a charismatic Christian convert named Hong Xiuquan. The rebellion was one of the largest civil wars in world history, and it lasted for more than a decade, causing immense destruction and loss of life.

The fall of the Qing Dynasty and the birth of the Republic of China

The late Qing Dynasty came to an end in 1912, when the last emperor, Puyi, was forced to abdicate. This marked the end of more than 2,000 years of imperial rule in China and the beginning of a new era, the Republic of China.

The Republic of China was established with the goal of modernizing the country and making it a more equal and democratic society. The first president of the Republic, Sun Yat-sen, was a visionary leader who advocated for constitutional democracy, social reform, and modernization. However, his efforts were hampered by the rise of powerful warlords who divided the country into rival factions, and the Republic was unable to achieve its goals of unity and stability.

In conclusion, the late Qing Dynasty was a period of great turmoil and change in China. The country was dominated by foreign powers, torn apart by civil war, and struggling to find its place in the modern world. Despite these challenges, however, the late Qing Dynasty laid the foundation for the Republic of China and set the stage for the country's transformation in the 20th century.

A. The Opium Wars and their impact on China

The Opium Wars, fought between China and Britain in the mid-19th century, marked a turning point in China's modern history and had a profound impact on the country's development.

The First Opium War (1839-1842) was triggered by China's efforts to halt the illegal trade of opium from British India into China. Despite a series of attempts to limit the opium trade, the British government viewed these efforts as a threat to its economic interests and responded with military force. The war ended with the Treaty of Nanking, which forced China to open its ports to foreign trade and cede control of Hong Kong to Britain.

The Second Opium War (1856-1860) was a continuation of the first, sparked by Chinese efforts to restrict the sale of opium and enforce the provisions of the Treaty of Nanking. The war resulted in a devastating defeat for China, with the country forced to accept even more concessions, including the legalization of opium and the expansion of foreign trade.

The impact of the Opium Wars on China was profound and far-reaching. The wars humiliated and weakened China, exposing the country's inability to resist foreign powers and its inability to protect its own sovereignty. This had a lasting impact on China's self-perception and national identity, fueling the rise of nationalism and anti-foreign sentiment.

The Opium Wars also had significant economic consequences for China, with the country forced to open its markets to foreign goods and cede control of key economic resources. This helped to further destabilize the Qing dynasty and set the stage for the country's ongoing modernization effort.

In conclusion, the Opium Wars marked a turning point in China's modern history, exposing the country's vulnerability to foreign influence and setting the stage for its ongoing modernization effort.

Opium Wars

The Opium Wars were two conflictual periods in the mid-19th century between China and foreign powers, particularly the United Kingdom and France. The First Opium War was triggered by the Chinese government's efforts to enforce its ban on opium trafficking by British merchants. The European forces' superior military power caused them to easily overpower the Chinese military, resulting in unequal treaties being imposed on China. These treaties allowed favourable tariffs, trade concessions, reparations, and ceded territory, as well as the opening of specified treaty ports (including Shanghai) to Western merchants. Additionally, Hong Kong was ceded to the British Empire, who maintained control of the region until 1997. During this period, the Chinese economy also weakened as a result of the wars, although the Taiping Rebellion and Dungan Revolt had a more prominent economic impact.

First Opium War

In the eighteenth century, China had a prosperous trade in porcelain, silk, and tea, exchanging them for silver with Europe. By the late 17th century, the British East India Company (EIC) had started to cultivate opium in the Bengal Presidency, which was then sold to private merchants who transported it to China for discreet sale. This saw an increase in opium use for recreational purposes, leading the Chinese government to ban the substance in 1729, 1799, 1814, and 1831. Nevertheless, smugglers and colluding Chinese officials continued to illegally import the drug, with American merchants smuggling it from Turkey, something that is now referred to as the Old China Trade. By 1833, more than 30,000 chests of opium were being sent to warehouses in the free-trade port of Canton. This eventually resulted in the First Opium War between China and Britain in 1839, which was fought over trading rights and diplomatic status.

In 1834, the British East India Company's monopoly over trade with China ended, leading to a surge in opium trading. In response, the Daoguang Emperor of the Qing Dynasty tasked Governor General Lin Zexu with ending the trade. Lin wrote an open letter to Queen Victoria pleading for her help in stopping the opium trade, which was later published in The Times. He also issued an edict which threatened serious punishments for opium smuggling. Charles Elliot, Chief Superintendent of British Trade in China, eventually entered Canton and paid for all the opium held by foreign governments and companies, which were then destroyed. After this, the British government decided to send a military expedition to China to impose reparations for financial losses and secure the opium trade. On 21 June 1840, a British naval force arrived at Macao and began to bombard the port of Dinghai.

In 1842, the Treaty of Nanjing marked the end of the war between China and Western powers. Under the agreement, Hong Kong Island and its surrounding areas were ceded to Britain. Five settlement ports - Shanghai, Canton, Ningbo, Fuzhou, and Xiamen (Amoy) - were established and opened to the Western traders. China was also required to pay a compensation of 21 million dollars to Britain for the destroyed opium, with six million to be paid immediately, and the rest in several installments. Another treaty in 1843 gave Britain the status of Most Favored Nation, and also included provisions for their extraterritoriality.

Second Opium War

In 1853, northern China was convulsed by the Taiping Rebellion, which established its capital at Nanking. In spite of this, a new Imperial Commissioner, Ye Mingchen, was appointed at Canton, determined to stamp out the opium trade, which was still technically illegal. In October 1856, he seized the Arrow, a ship claiming British registration, and threw its crew into chains. Sir John Bowring, Governor of British Hong Kong, called up Rear Admiral Sir Michael Seymour's East Indies and China Station fleet, which, on 23 October, bombarded and captured the Pearl River forts on the approach to Canton and proceeded to bombard Canton itself, but had insufficient forces to take and hold the city. On 15 December, during a riot in Canton, European commercial properties were set on fire and Bowring appealed for military intervention. The execution of a French missionary inspired support from France.

Britain and France now sought greater concessions from China, including the legalisation of the opium trade, expanding of the transportation of coolies to European colonies, opening all of China to British and French citizens and exempting foreign imports from internal transit duties.The war resulted in the 1858 Treaty of Tientsin, in which the Chinese government agreed to pay war reparations for the expenses of the recent conflict, open a second group of ten ports to European commerce, legalise the opium trade, and grant foreign traders and missionaries rights to travel within China. After a second phase of fighting which included the sack of the Old Summer Palace and the occupation of the Forbidden City palace complex in Beijing, the treaty was confirmed by the Convention of Peking in 1860

B. The Taiping Rebellion and its significance

The Taiping Rebellion was a significant conflict that took place in China during the mid-19th century, between the Qing dynasty and the Taiping Heavenly Kingdom, led by Hong Xiuquan. It lasted from 1850 to 1864, and resulted in the deaths of over 20 million people, making it one of the bloodiest wars in human history. Hong Xiuquan was an ethnic Hakka and claimed to be the brother of Jesus Christ, leading the uprising with the aim of converting the Han people to his version of Christianity, overthrowing the Qing dynasty, and transforming the state. The Taipings established a new state in Tianjing and gained control over a significant portion of southern China, with a population of nearly 30 million people. The war was characterized by extreme violence from both sides, with the Taipings committing widespread massacres against the Manchus and the Qing government engaging in massacres against the civilian population of the Taiping capital. The rebellion was eventually defeated by the Xiang Army, led by Zeng Guofan, which recaptured Nanjing after Hong Xiuquan's death in 1864. The civil war weakened the dynasty, but it also accelerated the rise of provincial power and may have foreshadowed the later loss of central control after the establishment of the Republic of China in 1912.

Origin

During the 19th century, the Qing dynasty in China faced several challenges, including famines, natural disasters, economic difficulties, and military defeats at the hands of foreign powers. This was caused by heavy taxation, rising rents, and increased poverty among farmers. The population of China had grown rapidly, while the government was becoming increasingly corrupt and weak, particularly in the southern regions where local clans dominated. These conditions led to an increase in banditry, secret societies, and self-defense units. The anti-Manchu sentiment was strongest among the Hakka community, a Han Chinese subgroup, and Christian missionaries were active.

Hong Huoxiu, a Hakka from Guangdong, was a poor farmer who had a dream about visiting heaven. In this dream, he discovered that he had a celestial family distinct from his earthly family and that he was meant to change his name. After several failed attempts at the imperial examination, Hong became interested in Christianity after reading pamphlets he had received from a missionary. He believed that these pamphlets gave him the key to interpreting his visions and that he was directed to rid the world of demons, including the corrupt Qing government and Confucian teachings. Hong went to Guangzhou to study the Bible with an American Baptist missionary, but he was not baptized. Roberts believed that Hong's followers were using religion for political purposes.

In 1844, after Hong started spreading his teachings, his follower Feng Yunshan established the God Worshipping Society, which followed Hong's blend of Christianity, Confucianism, Daoism, and indigenous millennial beliefs, which Hong portrayed as a revival of the old Chinese faith in Shangdi.

The historian states that the Taiping faith grew into a dynamic new Chinese religion called "Taiping Christianity".

Initially, the movement grew by controlling the activities of bandits and pirates in southern China in the late 1840s. However, the suppression of the movement by the Qing government led to the evolution of the movement into guerrilla warfare and eventually into a widespread civil war. Eventually, two other followers of the faith, Yang Xiuqing and Xiao Chaogui, claimed that they had the power to speak on behalf of the "Celestial Family", with Yang being considered the father and Xiao being considered Jesus Christ

Early years

The Taiping Rebellion was sparked by religious persecution of the God Worshipping Society by local officials in Guangxi. In response, Feng Yunshan and Wei Changhui organized a 10,000-strong rebel army who, in January 1851, managed to rout Qing forces stationed in Jintian. Taking advantage of their victory, Hong Xiuquan declared himself the Heavenly King of the Heavenly Kingdom of Peace in January 1851.

In the following year, the Taiping army marched north to Hunan, where they captured Changsha, Yuezhou and Wuchang. By 1853, they had reached the Yangtze River and captured Anqing. It is suspected that the Taiping leadership had reached out to the Triad organizations to recruit more troops, as they had used titles similar to those of the Triads. However, this relationship deteriorated after the capture of Nanjing in 1852.

Middle years

On March 19, 1853, the Taipings took the city of Nanjing, declaring it the Heavenly Capital, and then proceeded to kill all the Manchu men and burn the Manchu women alive outside the city. Following this, the Taiping army launched two expeditions, a northern and a western one, with the latter achieving some success. After this, Hong Xiuquan isolated himself from the policies and administration of his kingdom, living in luxury with many women and issuing religious edicts. His relationship with Yang Xiuqing deteriorated, culminating in the 1856 Tianjing Incident where Yang and his followers were massacred at Hong's orders.

Shi Dakai's refusal to participate in the killing of his family and retinue by Wei and Qin resulted in the latter's execution of Wei and Qin. As a reward, he was given control of five Taiping armies which were consolidated into one. Fearing for his life, Shi Dakai fled Tianjing to Sichuan. With Hong and Yang out of the equation, the remaining Taiping leaders attempted to gain wider support and alliances with European powers but were unsuccessful. Inside China, the rebellion encountered hostility from the traditional rural classes due to their aversion to Chinese customs and Confucian values, while the upper class, who were uncomfortable with the Taiping ideology and the policy of separation of the sexes, sided with the Qing forces. Zeng Guofan's Xiang Army fought for the Qing against the Taiping and managed to push back the Taiping's advance in the western theater, eventually reclaiming much of Hubei and Jiangxi provinces. In December 1856, the Qing forces recaptured Wuchang, and in May 1858, the Xiang Army seized Jiujiang. Lastly, the entirety of Jiangxi province was taken back in September.

In 1859, following the recruitment of his cousin Hong Rengan, Hong Xiuquan was able to gain considerable power in the Taiping forces in Nanjing. Hong Rengan then proposed an expansion plan for the Taiping Heavenly Kingdom. This plan led to successful invasions of the Jiangsu and Zhejiang provinces, which were the most affluent parts of the Qing Empire. The Taiping forces managed to take Hangzhou on March 19, 1860, Changzhou on May 26th, and Suzhou on June 2nd. During this time, Zeng's forces moved south along the Yangtze River.

Fall of the Taiping Heavenly Kingdom

In August 1860, a Qing army supported by European officers, led by Frederick Townsend Ward, managed to repel an attempt to take Shanghai. This army would later become known as the "Ever Victorious Army," a highly experienced and well-trained military force commanded by Charles George Gordon. In 1861, the Xiang Army, under Zeng Guofan, with assistance from the Royal Navy, took Anqing. Later that same year the Taipings made their final Eastern Expedition, successfully capturing Ningbo in December, and Hangzhou by the end of the year. They surrounded Shanghai in January of 1862, but were unable to take the city. The Ever Victorious Army managed to repel them and also assisted in defending other treaty ports, such as Ningbo, which was retaken in May 10th. Additionally, they aided imperial troops in regaining Taiping strongholds along the Yangtze River. By 1863, Shi Dakai had surrendered to the Qing, was executed, and the Qing reconquest had begun in earnest. Zeng Guofan, Zuo Zongtang, and Li Hongzhang led loyal troops in regaining control of most areas by early 1864.

In 1862, the Xiang Army began besieging Nanjing, but were unable to overcome the Taiping Army. Unfortunately, Hong Xiuquan, who had declared that God would protect the city, died of food poisoning after the city ran low on food supplies. After his death, Qing forces took the city and Hong's body was buried in the former Ming Imperial Palace, only to be later exhumed and cremated. Four months before the fall of the Taiping Heavenly Kingdom, Hong Xiuquan abdicated in favor of his eldest son and resistance was gradually pushed into the highlands of Jiangxi, Zhejiang, Fujian and Guangdong. On January 29, 1866, the last Taiping loyalist, Wang Haiyang, was defeated, effectively ending the Taiping Rebellion.

Aftermath

The fall of Nanjing in 1864 marked the destruction of the Taiping regime, though several hundred thousand Taiping troops still continued the fight. It wasn't until 1871 that the last Taiping army was wiped out by government forces in the border region of Hunan, Guizhou and Guangxi. The Taiping wars also spilled over into Vietnam, with Wu Lingyun proclaiming himself the King of Dingling in the Sino-Vietnamese border region. This was destroyed during a Qing campaign in 1868, and his son Wu Yazhong, also called Wu Kun, was killed in 1869. As a result, Wu Kun's troops broke up and became marauding armies such as the Yellow Flag Army and the Black Flag Army. These "Flag Gangs" eventually disbanded and became bandit groups that plundered remnants of the Lan Xang kingdom, which were then engaged in combat against the forces of King Rama V until 1890. These conflicts were misnamed "Haw wars" as the victims did not know where the bandits had come from, and mistook them for Chinese Muslims from Yunnan.

Death toll

With no reliable census at the time, estimates of the death toll of the Taiping Rebellion are speculative. The most widely cited sources estimate the total number of deaths during the almost 14 years of the rebellion to be approximately 20–30 million civilians and soldiers. Most of the deaths were attributed to plague and famine. Some analysts have claimed that the death toll may have reached 100 million.

Concurrent rebellions

The Nian Rebellion of 1853 to 1868 and the Panthay Rebellion of 1855 to 1873 in the southwest, as well as the Dungan Revolt of 1862 to 1876 in the northwest, posed serious problems for the Qing Dynasty. Former Taiping soldiers and commanders, such as Lai Wenguang, joined forces with the Nians during the Taiping Rebellion's decline. In addition, remnant forces from the Red Turban Rebellion, the Small Swords Society Uprising, and the Li Yonghe and Lan Chaoding Rebellion combined with the Taiping army. Du Wenxiu, the leader of the Panthay Rebellion in Yunnan, sought to overthrow the Qing government and had contact with the Taiping Heavenly Kingdom. His forces were comprised of Han Chinese, Li, Bai, and Hani peoples, as well as non-Muslim tribes such as the Shan and Kakhyen. The Dungan Revolt, however, was not an attempt to overthrow the Qing Dynasty, as its leader Ma Hualong had accepted an imperial title. More so, it was a result of intersectional fighting between Muslim factions and Han Chinese, with various groups fighting without any unified goal. In 1862, the Dungan Rebellion did not start with a specific plan but was instead a combination of several small fights and riots caused by misinformation, including the false belief that the Hui Muslims were helping the Taiping. Ma Xiaoshi, a Hui Muslim, claimed that the Shaanxi Muslim

Rebellion was tied to the Taiping. Historian Jonathan Spence suggested that the Taiping's ultimate downfall was that it could not successfully coordinate with other uprisings.

C. The fall of the Qing Dynasty and the birth of the Republic of China

The fall of the Qing dynasty in 1911 marked the end of China's imperial era and the birth of the Republic of China. The collapse of the dynasty was the result of a number of factors, including political corruption, economic instability, and foreign influence.

The late 19th and early 20th centuries were marked by a series of reforms and modernization efforts aimed at revitalizing the Qing dynasty. However, these efforts were not enough to stem the growing tide of unrest and discontent among the Chinese people. In addition, China's defeat in the First Sino-Japanese War (1894-1895) and the Boxer Rebellion (1899-1901) further weakened the Qing dynasty and fueled anti-foreign sentiment.

The final straw came in 1911, when a series of uprisings and mutinies broke out across the country. The uprising was led by Sun Yat-sen, a nationalist and reformer who sought to establish a democratic republic in China. With the support of the military, Sun and his followers were able to overthrow the Qing dynasty and establish the Republic of China.

The birth of the Republic of China marked a new era in Chinese history. The new government was democratic in form, with a president, a cabinet, and a national assembly. However, the new republic was plagued by political instability, economic turmoil, and military conflict, as various warlords and regional powers vied for control of the country.

In conclusion, the fall of the Qing dynasty and the birth of the Republic of China marked a turning point in China's modern history. The establishment of the republic represented a significant step forward for China, as the country transitioned from an imperial system to a democratic one. However, the new republic faced a number of challenges and obstacles, including political instability, economic turmoil, and military conflict, which would shape China's development in the decades to come.

III. THE REPUBLIC OF CHINA (1912-1949)

The Republic of China (1912-1949) was a period of political and social turmoil in China, marked by political instability, economic decline, and military conflict. Despite its many challenges, the period was also characterized by efforts to modernize and reform the country, as well as the growth of nationalism and anti-foreign sentiment.

One of the biggest challenges faced by the Republic of China was the fragmentation of the country into various regions controlled by different warlords. This political instability was compounded by economic decline, as the country struggled to cope with the aftermath of World War I and the global economic depression of the 1930s.

In the 1920s and 1930s, the Republic of China saw a resurgence of nationalism and anti-foreign sentiment. This was fueled in part by the May Fourth Movement, a mass protest movement that sought to reform the country and promote national pride.

In addition to the political and social challenges faced by the Republic of China, the country was also threatened by external forces, including the expansion of Japan in Asia and the communist movement led by Mao Zedong. In 1937, Japan launched a full-scale invasion of China, which marked the beginning of the Second Sino-Japanese War.

The war with Japan had a profound impact on China, as the country was devastated by the conflict and its resources were depleted. After the end of the war, the country was left vulnerable to the communist forces led by Mao, who declared the establishment of the People's Republic of China in 1949.

In conclusion, the Republic of China (1912-1949) was a period of political, social, and economic turmoil, marked by political instability, economic decline, and military conflict. Despite its many challenges, the period was also characterized by efforts to modernize and reform the country, as well as the growth of nationalism and anti-foreign sentiment. The legacy of the Republic of China continues to shape China's development to this day.

A. Sun Yat-sen and the Nationalist Party

Sun Yat-sen was a Chinese revolutionary and statesman who played a pivotal role in the fall of the Qing dynasty and the establishment of the Republic of China. Sun was born in 1866 in Guangdong province and grew up in a time of great social and political upheaval in China. He was educated in Hawaii and Hong Kong and later travelled to the United States and Europe, where he was exposed to the ideas of democracy and nationalism.

Sun returned to China in the 1890s and became a leader of the revolutionary movement. He founded the Nationalist Party, also known as the Kuomintang, in 1912. The Nationalist Party was dedicated to overthrowing the Qing dynasty and establishing a democratic republic in China.

Under Sun's leadership, the Nationalist Party played a key role in the fall of the Qing dynasty and the establishment of the Republic of China. After the fall of the dynasty, Sun became the first provisional president of the new republic, but he was soon forced to resign due to political opposition.

Sun Yat-sen died in 1925, but his legacy lived on through the Nationalist Party, which remained a powerful force in Chinese politics for many years. The party was led by Chiang Kai-shek after Sun's death and played a central role in the political, social, and economic development of China in the decades that followed.

In conclusion, Sun Yat-sen was a key figure in the modern history of China, playing a crucial role in the fall of the Qing dynasty and the establishment of the Republic of China. His ideas and vision, as well as the political movement he founded, the Nationalist Party, continue to influence China's development to this day.

B. The Warlord Era and its effects on China

The Warlord Era was a period in the history of China that lasted from 1916 to 1928, during which the country was fragmented into various regions controlled by different warlords. This political instability was the result of the fall of the Qing dynasty and the weak central government that emerged in its place.

During the Warlord Era, the warlords who controlled different regions of China were more concerned with maintaining their own power and territory than with the welfare of the country as a whole. This led to frequent wars and conflicts between the warlords, which further weakened the central government and destabilized the country.

In addition to the political instability, the Warlord Era was characterized by economic decline and widespread poverty. The warlords were often more interested in exploiting the resources of their territories than in promoting economic growth and development, and as a result, many regions of the country remained poor and underdeveloped.

The Warlord Era had a profound impact on the future of China, as it contributed to the weakening of the central government and the growth of nationalism and anti-foreign sentiment. The period also saw the rise of the Communist Party of China, which emerged as a major political force in the country during this time.

In conclusion, the Warlord Era was a period of political instability and economic decline in China, marked by the fragmentation of the country into various regions controlled by different warlords. The period had a profound impact on the future of China, contributing to the weakening of the central government and the growth of nationalism and anti-foreign sentiment, and setting the stage for the rise of the Communist Party of China.

C. The rise of the Communist Party of China

The Communist Party of China (CPC) was founded in 1921, during the Warlord Era, as a political party dedicated to the establishment of a socialist state in China. The party was initially a small and marginal organisation, but it grew rapidly in the 1920s and 1930s as the country was beset by political instability and economic decline.

The CPC's growth was aided by its close association with the Soviet Union, which provided financial and ideological support to the party. The CPC also attracted a growing number of supporters by advocating for social and economic reforms that would benefit the working class and the poor, who had been marginalized and exploited by the warlords and the Nationalist Party.

In the late 1920s, the CPC launched an armed uprising against the Nationalist Party, known as the Chinese Civil War, which lasted for several years. The CPC eventually emerged victorious in 1949, after several years of intense fighting, and established the People's Republic of China, with Mao Zedong as its first chairman.

The rise of the CPC marked a major turning point in the modern history of China, as the party established a one-party socialist state that would dominate Chinese politics and society for many years to come. The CPC's rise also had significant implications for the rest of the world, as China became one of the largest and most influential countries in the world, and a major player in international affairs.

In conclusion, the rise of the Communist Party of China was a major turning point in the modern history of China, marking the establishment of a one-party socialist state that would dominate Chinese politics and society for many years to come. The CPC's rise also had significant implications for the rest of the world, as China became one of the largest and most influential countries in the world, and a major player in international affairs.

IV. THE PEOPLE'S REPUBLIC OF CHINA (1949-PRESENT)

The People's Republic of China (PRC) was established in 1949, after the Communist Party of China (CPC) emerged victorious in the Chinese Civil War. The PRC was founded on the principles of socialism and was intended to be a democratic and socialist state, with the CPC as the sole legal political party.

In the early years of the PRC, the country underwent significant social and economic transformations, as the CPC implemented a series of reforms aimed at modernizing the economy, improving living standards, and increasing political control. The party also launched campaigns to improve education, public health, and the status of women and minority groups.

In the late 1950s, the CPC launched the Great Leap Forward, a series of reforms aimed at rapidly modernizing the economy and improving living standards. The reforms, however, proved to be a disaster, leading to widespread famine and economic decline. The CPC later launched the Cultural Revolution in 1966, a decade-long political and social upheaval aimed at purging the country of perceived enemies of the revolution and promoting the ideals of communism. The Cultural Revolution had a profound impact on Chinese society and resulted in widespread social and economic disruption.

In the late 1970s and early 1980s, the CPC launched a series of reforms aimed at modernizing the economy and increasing economic growth. These reforms, known as the Reform and Opening-Up Policy, were led by Deng Xiaoping and proved to be highly successful, leading to a period of rapid economic growth and increased prosperity in China.

In recent years, the PRC has become one of the largest and most powerful countries in the world, with a rapidly growing economy and a significant military presence. The country has also become more active in international affairs, playing a major role in shaping the global political and economic landscape.

In conclusion, the People's Republic of China has been a major player in the modern history of the world, undergoing significant social, economic, and political transformations since its founding in 1949. The PRC has become one of the largest and most powerful countries in the world, with a rapidly growing economy and a significant military presence, and is now a major player in international affairs.

A. Mao Zedong and the Communist Revolution

Mao Zedong was the founding father of the People's Republic of China (PRC) and one of the most influential leaders of the Communist Party of China (CPC). Mao was born in Hunan province in 1893 and became a Marxist in the 1920s. He later became a leader of the CPC and was instrumental in the Communist victory in the Chinese Civil War, which led to the establishment of the PRC in 1949.

Mao is best known for his role in the Communist Revolution, which aimed to transform China into a socialist state. He launched a series of reforms and campaigns aimed at improving living standards, increasing political control, and modernizing the economy. The most famous of these campaigns was the Great Leap Forward, which was launched in the late 1950s. The reforms, however, proved to be a disaster, leading to widespread famine and economic decline.

In 1966, Mao launched the Cultural Revolution, a decade-long political and social upheaval aimed at purging the country of perceived enemies of the revolution and promoting the ideals of communism. The Cultural Revolution had a profound impact on Chinese society and resulted in widespread social and economic disruption.

Despite the many challenges and setbacks that Mao faced during his time in power, he remains a highly controversial and influential figure in modern Chinese history. Mao's legacy is a mixed one, with some regard him as a visionary and others viewing him as a ruthless dictator.

In conclusion, Mao Zedong was a key figure in the Communist Revolution in China and played a major role in the establishment of the People's Republic of China. Despite the many challenges and setbacks he faced, Mao remains a highly influential figure in modern Chinese history and his legacy continues to shape the country today.

B. The Cultural Revolution and its aftermath

The Cultural Revolution was a decade-long political and social upheaval launched by Mao Zedong in 1966. Its goal was to purge the country of perceived enemies of the revolution and promote the ideals of communism. The campaign was characterized by widespread political and social turmoil, with millions of people being persecuted, imprisoned, or killed.

The Cultural Revolution had a profound impact on Chinese society, resulting in widespread social and economic disruption. The country's educational system was disrupted, with many schools and universities being closed. Cultural heritage was also targeted, with historic buildings and artifacts being destroyed.

After Mao's death in 1976, the Cultural Revolution was officially declared over by his successor, Deng Xiaoping. Deng launched a series of reforms aimed at modernizing the economy and restoring stability to the country. These reforms, known as the Four Modernizations, helped to revive China's economy and paved the way for the country's transformation into a major economic power.

Despite the many challenges and setbacks that followed the Cultural Revolution, China emerged from this period of turmoil as a more stable and prosperous nation. The country has since continued to experience rapid economic growth and has become a major player on the world stage.

In conclusion, the Cultural Revolution was a defining period in modern Chinese history, characterized by widespread political and social upheaval. Despite the many challenges and setbacks it brought, the Cultural Revolution helped to lay the foundation for the country's transformation into a modern, prosperous nation.

C. Reform and Opening Up under Deng Xiaoping

Deng Xiaoping was a Chinese statesman and political leader who served as the Premier of the People's Republic of China from 1978 to 1983. He is widely regarded as the architect of China's economic reform and modernization.

After Mao's death in 1976, Deng emerged as the country's top leader and launched a series of reforms aimed at modernizing the economy and restoring stability to the country. These reforms, known as the Four Modernizations, focused on agriculture, industry, science and technology, and national defense.

The centerpiece of Deng's reforms was the policy of "reform and opening up." This policy was aimed at opening China's economy to the outside world and encouraging investment and entrepreneurship. In 1978, the first Special Economic Zones (SEZs) were established in the country, providing foreign investors with tax incentives and other benefits. This policy proved to be highly successful, and helped to revive China's economy and spur rapid economic growth.

Under Deng's leadership, China transformed into a major economic power, becoming the world's second-largest economy by the end of the 20th century. The country's success has been driven by a combination of factors, including a rapidly growing population, a large pool of cheap labour, and a favourable investment climate.

In conclusion, Deng Xiaoping was a key figure in modern Chinese history and played a major role in the country's transformation into a modern, prosperous nation. His policy of "reform and opening up" helped to revive China's economy and paved the way for the country's rapid economic growth and development.

D. The 21st century and China's rise as a global power.

In the early 21st century, China's rise as a global power continued at an unprecedented pace. The country's economy continued to grow rapidly, and by the end of the first decade of the century, China had become the world's second-largest economy.

As China's economic power has grown, so too has its political and military influence. The country has increasingly taken on a more prominent role in international affairs, and has been increasingly assertive in pursuing its national interests.

One of the most visible manifestations of China's rise as a global power has been its increasing military might. The country has been modernizing its armed forces, and has invested heavily in new weapons and technologies. This has enabled China to play a more active role in global security affairs and to project its power further beyond its borders.

Another area where China has increasingly asserted itself is in trade. The country has become a major player in global trade and has been an influential voice in international trade negotiations. In recent years, China has also launched several major infrastructure projects, including the Belt and Road Initiative, aimed at increasing its influence and boosting economic growth across Asia and beyond.

In conclusion, China's rise as a global power in the 21st century has been one of the most significant developments of our time. With its growing economic and military might and increasing assertiveness on the world stage, China is set to play an increasingly influential role in shaping the future of our planet.

Economic Growth:

The book could examine the factors that have driven China's rapid economic growth over the past few decades, including its opening up to the global economy and its investment in infrastructure and technology. It could also discuss the challenges that China faces in sustaining its economic growth, such as declining demographics and mounting debt levels.

Yes, exploring the drivers and challenges of China's economic growth is a crucial aspect of understanding its rise as a global power. In addition to the factors you mentioned, the book could also explore the following:

State-led Capitalism:

State-led capitalism is an economic system where the state plays a dominant role in guiding and directing economic development, typically through state-owned enterprises (SOEs) and other forms of government intervention. In state-led capitalism, the state takes a proactive role in promoting economic growth and shaping the business environment, rather than relying solely on market forces to drive development.

In the context of China, state-led capitalism refers to the government's active role in driving economic growth and development through SOEs and other forms of intervention. This has been a key aspect of China's rise as an economic power and has helped to spur rapid growth in a number of industries, including manufacturing, infrastructure, and high-tech.

However, state-led capitalism has also been criticized for creating a number of challenges and inefficiencies, such as crony capitalism, corruption, and an uneven playing field for private enterprises. Additionally, some argue that the dominance of SOEs has stifled innovation and competition and that the government's heavy hand in the economy has limited the ability of market forces to determine the allocation of resources.

Despite these criticisms, state-led capitalism has remained a central aspect of China's economic development and has helped to drive the country's rapid growth and modernization over the past few decades.

Labor Market:

The labor market refers to the system in which workers are hired and employed, and in which wages and working conditions are determined. The labor market is a crucial component of any economy, as it determines the allocation of labor resources and the level of economic activity.

In China, the labor market has undergone significant changes in recent decades, reflecting the country's rapid economic growth and modernization. In the early years of the People's Republic, the labor market was highly centralized, with the state controlling the allocation of jobs and setting wages. However, since the start of the Reform and Opening Up policy in the late 1970s, the labor market has become increasingly decentralized and market-driven, with private enterprises and foreign firms playing an increasingly important role in job creation and wage determination.

Despite these changes, the labor market in China remains shaped by a number of unique features, including a large and growing pool of rural migrant workers, an aging population, and a highly competitive job market in certain cities and industries. Additionally, issues such as wage stagnation, income inequality, and labor rights abuses remain pressing challenges for the Chinese labor market.

Overall, the labour market in China continues to evolve and develop, reflecting the broader changes and challenges facing the country as it strives to maintain its rapid economic growth and increase its global competitiveness.

Export-oriented Growth:

Export-oriented growth is an economic strategy that focuses on increasing a country's exports as a means of boosting economic growth and development. This approach is based on the idea that expanding exports will increase demand for a country's products, create jobs, and stimulate investment and innovation.

In the case of China, export-oriented growth has been a key driver of the country's rapid economic development since the start of its Reform and Opening Up policy in the late 1970s. The Chinese government has actively encouraged the growth of its export sector through a variety of measures, including investment in infrastructure, tax incentives for export-oriented firms, and the development of special economic zones to promote foreign investment.

As a result of these efforts, China has become one of the world's largest exporters, with exports accounting for a significant share of the country's gross domestic product (GDP) and employment. However, the country's dependence on exports has also created new challenges and vulnerabilities, including increased competition from other developing countries and rising concerns over trade imbalances and currency issues.

Overall, export-oriented growth has been a major contributor to China's economic success in recent decades, but the country will need to find ways to address these challenges if it is to continue its rise as a global economic power.

Innovation:

Innovation refers to the development and introduction of new ideas, products, and processes that create value and improve efficiency. In the context of economic growth and development, innovation is seen as a key driver of competitiveness and productivity.

In China, innovation has played a significant role in the country's rapid economic growth in recent decades. The Chinese government has recognized the importance of innovation and has made it a central part of its development strategy, investing heavily in research and development (R&D), science and technology, and education.

As a result of these efforts, China has made impressive gains in a number of high-tech industries, such as information technology, biotechnology, and renewable energy. The country has also emerged as a global leader in innovation, with many of its companies, such as Huawei, ZTE, and Tencent, becoming household names in the tech industry.

However, despite these advances, China still faces a number of challenges in its quest to become an innovation-led economy, including a lack of intellectual property protection, limited access to high-quality research and development inputs, and a shortage of skilled workers.

Overall, innovation has been a key contributor to China's economic success in recent decades, and the country will need to continue to prioritize innovation if it is to maintain its position as a leading global economy.

Global Influence:
China has used its growing economic and military power to influence international affairs. This could include its role in the global trade system, its relationship with major powers such as the United States and Russia, and its efforts to increase its soft power through cultural exchanges and diplomacy.
The Belt and Road Initiative: The book could examine China's ambitious infrastructure project, which aims to connect countries across Asia, Europe, and Africa. It could discuss the goals behind the initiative and the challenges that China faces in executing it.
examining China's growing global influence is another important aspect of understanding its rise as a world power. In addition to the topics you mentioned, the book could also explore the following:

The Belt and Road Initiative:

The Belt and Road Initiative (BRI) is a development strategy and framework proposed by the Chinese government in 2013 that aims to enhance connectivity and cooperation between countries in Asia, Europe, and Africa through infrastructure development, trade and investment. The initiative encompasses two main components: the "Silk Road Economic Belt," which focuses on connecting China with Europe through Central and Western Asia, and the "21st Century Maritime Silk Road," which aims to connect China with Southeast Asia, Africa, and Europe.

The initiative aims to create new trade routes and markets for Chinese goods, as well as expand its economic influence in the region. The BRI includes the construction of ports, railways, highways, and other infrastructure projects, as well as financial investment and support for participating countries.

While the initiative has been embraced by many countries in the region, it has also faced criticism, particularly from Western countries, who view it as an attempt by China to increase its influence and assert its dominance in the region. Additionally, some participating countries have raised concerns over the sustainability of the loans provided by China and the impact of the initiative on their own economies.

Overall, the Belt and Road Initiative is a major initiative that has the potential to significantly impact the economic and political landscape in the region and beyond.

Military Modernization:

Military modernization refers to the process of improving and updating a country's military capabilities, including its weapons, equipment, and strategies. The primary goal of military modernization is to enhance a country's ability to defend its national interests and maintain security.

In the case of China, its military modernization has been a major aspect of its rise as a global power. Over the past few decades, China has invested heavily in its military, modernizing its armed forces, improving its command and control structures, and developing its capability to project power beyond its borders.

China's military modernization has been driven by a number of factors, including its efforts to defend its national interests, secure its maritime and territorial claims, and participate in peacekeeping operations. Additionally, China has invested in advanced technologies, such as artificial intelligence, cyber capabilities, and unmanned systems, in order to enhance its military capabilities.

The implications of China's military modernization are far-reaching and have important implications for regional and global security. On one hand, China's military modernization has improved its ability to defend its national interests and maintain regional stability. On the other hand, it has also raised concerns among its neighbours and other major powers, particularly the United States, about the balance of power in Asia and the impact of China's military development on regional and global security.

Multilateral Institutions:

Multilateral institutions refer to international organizations that are made up of multiple countries working together to achieve common goals. These institutions can take many forms, including intergovernmental organizations, international financial institutions, and global governance bodies.

In the case of China, its participation in multilateral institutions has been an important aspect of its rise as a global power. China has sought to use these institutions to advance its interests and increase its influence on the global stage.

For example, China has become an increasingly active participant in the United Nations, using its role in the organization to promote its interests and shape global governance. It has also become a major player in the World Trade Organization, working to advance trade liberalization and increase its economic influence.

Additionally, China has established its own multilateral institutions, such as the Asian Infrastructure Investment Bank and the Belt and Road Initiative, as a means of promoting its economic interests and increasing its influence in the region.

The impact of China's participation in multilateral institutions has been significant, as it has helped to reshape the global order and increase China's influence in international affairs. However, its increasing influence has also raised concerns among some countries and international institutions about the balance of power and the implications of China's rise to global governance.

Soft Power:

Soft power is a concept in international relations that refers to the ability of a country to influence others through attraction and persuasion, rather than coercion or force. Soft power is based on a country's cultural, political, and economic appeal, and can be an effective means of achieving international goals and advancing national interests.

China has been actively working to build its soft power in recent years, as it seeks to increase its influence on the global stage. This has involved a number of initiatives aimed at enhancing China's cultural appeal, such as hosting international cultural events and promoting Chinese culture abroad.

Additionally, China has sought to use its economic power and its investments in infrastructure and development projects to increase its soft power. For example, the Belt and Road Initiative, which is a massive infrastructure project that spans multiple countries, has been seen as an effort by China to increase its soft power and economic influence in the region.

The impact of China's soft power efforts has been significant, as it has helped to enhance the country's image and reputation on the global stage. However, some have criticized China's soft power initiatives as being an attempt to "mask" its more authoritarian and repressive policies, and there is an ongoing debate about the true effectiveness of soft power in advancing national interests.

Political Systems:
The political system in China during modern times has been unique in many ways. The Communist Party of China has been the only ruling party since 1949, and it has exercised authoritarian control over the media and civil society. The state has played a significant role in the economy, with state-owned enterprises dominating key industries and the government playing a major role in guiding economic development. Despite this, there have been significant challenges, such as corruption and social unrest, which have arisen in recent years. These challenges have highlighted the need for greater political openness and transparency, as well as the need to balance stability with greater political freedom. The political system plays a crucial role in China's rise as a global power, as it allows for long-term planning and decision-making and helps to maintain stability and order. This has allowed China to pursue its strategic goals and assert its influence on the global stage.

Social Changes:

China has undergone significant social changes in recent decades, including urbanization and the growth of the middle class. Urbanization has led to the migration of millions of people from rural areas to cities and has transformed China into a predominantly urban society. The growth of the middle class has increased consumer spending and fueled the development of new industries, such as the service sector. The transformation of gender roles, with increasing numbers of women entering the workforce, has also had a profound impact on society.

However, these changes have also created challenges, such as income inequality and the strain on social services and infrastructure in cities. The impact on the family and traditional values has been significant, and there is concern about the effect of rapid change on social stability. Nevertheless, these changes have also contributed to China's rise as a global power, such as through the growth of its consumer market and the increasing influence of its popular culture. The book could explore the interplay between these social changes and China's rise, and could provide insights into how the country is adapting to these changes and the challenges it faces in the future.

Regional Tensions:

Regional tensions refer to conflicts and disputes that exist between different regions within a country or between countries in a specific region. In the case of China, there are a number of regional tensions have arisen in recent times.

One of the main sources of regional tensions in China is territorial disputes in the South and East China Seas. These disputes involve a number of countries, including China, Japan, the Philippines, and Vietnam, and centre around the control of islands and maritime boundaries in these waters. These disputes have led to heightened tensions and have the potential to escalate into conflict, which could have major implications for the stability of the region and for China's relationships with other countries in the region.

Another source of regional tension in China is its relationship with Taiwan. The island has a separate government and its own political and economic system, which China views as a breakaway province that must eventually be reunified with the mainland. The tension between China and Taiwan has a significant impact on the stability of the region and on China's relationships with other countries in the region.

Finally, there are also tensions between the coastal and inland regions of China. The coastal regions, which are home to many of China's largest cities and its most advanced industries, have been the engines of the country's economic growth in recent decades. However, the inland regions, which are less developed, have been left behind, leading to growing disparities between the two regions and causing social and political tensions.

Overall, the regional tensions in China have a major impact on the stability of the region and on China's relationships with other countries in the region. They also have implications for China's rise as a global power, as they can affect its ability to pursue its strategic goals and to maintain stability and stability while pursuing its strategic objectives. The book could critically examine the various regional tensions in China, including the factors that have contributed to their emergence, the ways in which they have been addressed, and the impact that they have had on China and the region.

V. DOMESTIC POLICIES AND REFORMS:

The book could critically analyse the domestic policies and reforms implemented by the Chinese government in order to support its rise as a global power. The examination would include an analysis of the reasons behind these reforms, such as the need to address economic imbalances, promote innovation, and respond to social and political pressures. The implementation of these reforms would also be explored, including the role of different actors like the central government, local governments, and the private sector.

The book would also assess the effectiveness of these reforms in achieving their intended goals, taking into account the impact they have had on various aspects of Chinese society, such as economic growth, social stability, and environmental sustainability. The challenges that the government faces in continuing to implement these reforms would be discussed, such as resistance from entrenched interests, rising public expectations, and the need to maintain political stability.

Furthermore, the book would consider the implications of these reforms for China's rise as a global power, including their impact on the economy, relationships with other countries, and standing in the international community. The examination would be done in a critical manner, taking into account the strengths and weaknesses of the reforms, and the potential trade-offs involved in implementing them. The book could critically analyze the domestic policies and reforms implemented by the Chinese government in support of its rise as a global power. This analysis would involve examining the reasons behind the reforms, including factors such as the need to address economic imbalances, promote innovation, and respond to social and political pressures. The book would delve into the process of implementing these reforms, including the role played by various actors such as the central government, local governments, and the private sector. The book would also evaluate the effectiveness of these reforms in meeting their intended goals, and the impact that they have had on various aspects of Chinese society, such as economic growth, social stability, and environmental sustainability. The book would consider the challenges that the government faces in continuing to implement these reforms, such as resistance from entrenched interests, rising public expectations, and the need to maintain political stability. Finally, the book would examine the implications of these reforms for China's rise as a global power, including the impact on its economy, its relationships with other countries, and its standing in the international community.

VI. CHINA'S RELATIONSHIPS WITH MAJOR POWERS:

The book could examine China's relationships with major powers, including the United States, Russia, and the European Union. It could analyze the drivers behind these relationships, such as economic interdependence, strategic interests, and political differences. The book could also consider the current state of these relationships, including areas of cooperation and competition, and the impact that they have on China's rise as a global power. Additionally, the book could explore the potential for these relationships to evolve in the future, including the possibility of closer cooperation or heightened tensions. The book could also examine the implications of China's relationships with major powers for the international system, including the impact on global governance, the distribution of power, and the stability of the international order. The book could critically analyze these relationships and their dynamics, considering the different perspectives and interests of each party, and the impact of broader international trends and events.

A. China and U.S

The relationship between the United States and China is one of the most significant bilateral relationships in the world, shaping global politics and economics. Since the 1970s, when President Richard Nixon visited China and re-established diplomatic ties, the relationship has undergone numerous ups and downs, reflecting changes in both the domestic and international context of each country.

During the Cold War, the relationship was defined by a strategic partnership, as both countries sought to counter the Soviet Union. However, this relationship was tested by a range of issues, including human rights abuses in China, differences over trade, and tensions in the Taiwan Strait. In recent years, the relationship has become increasingly strained, with disagreements over issues such as trade, intellectual property, and the South China Sea, as well as growing concerns over China's rise as a global power.

Despite these challenges, the relationship remains one of the most important in the world, reflecting the interdependence of the two countries on economic, political, and strategic levels. The United States and China are two of the largest economies in the world, with significant trade and investment ties, and their relationship has a significant impact on global economic stability. In addition, the relationship is critical for international security, as both countries have a major role to play in addressing regional and global security challenges, such as the proliferation of weapons of mass destruction, climate change, and terrorism.

As the world continues to evolve, the relationship between the United States and China is likely to continue to evolve and be shaped by a range of factors, including changes in domestic politics, the dynamics of the international system, and the emergence of new challenges and opportunities. The ability of both countries to manage these changes and navigate their relationship in a constructive and cooperative manner will have a major impact on the future stability and prosperity of the Asia-Pacific region and the world as a whole.

B. China and Russia

Despite the strengthening relationship between China and Russia in recent years, there are also some potential issues that may cause difficulty in the future. One of the biggest concerns is the political differences between the two countries. Although both countries have generally agreed on many global issues, there are still some disagreements on certain policies. For example, Russia has taken a more conservative approach to foreign affairs, while China has taken a more liberal stance. This could create tension between the two countries if the differences become more pronounced. Additionally, economic disparities between the two countries could also create problems. China's economy is much larger than Russia's and this could lead to competition and disagreement over resources. Finally, the rising military power of China has caused some consternation in Russia, as the former has become increasingly assertive in the international arena.

Overall, the relationship between China and Russia is positive and mutually beneficial. However, there are some potential areas of disagreement that could cause issues in the future. It is important for both countries to continue to engage in positive dialogue and to take a proactive stance in addressing potential issues that may arise. With an open and honest approach, China and Russia can ensure the friendship between them is strong and beneficial for both countries.

C. China and the European Union,

The book could examine the relationship between China and the European Union, including the economic, political, and strategic aspects of this relationship. This could include an analysis of the trade and investment ties between the two sides, as well as the challenges posed by issues such as competition for resources, security concerns, and differing values and interests. The book could also consider the efforts made by both sides to enhance cooperation, such as through diplomatic and economic engagement, and the impact that these efforts have had on their relationship. Additionally, the book could explore the impact of the relationship between China and the European Union on the international community, including the implications for global governance and the stability of the international order. The book could also examine the challenges facing the relationship in the future, such as rising competition and tensions, and the potential for cooperation in areas such as technology and climate change.

VII. THE BELT AND ROAD INITIATIVE:

The Belt and Road Initiative (BRI), also known as the One Belt, One Road (OBOR) or the Belt and Road, is a development strategy and framework launched by the Chinese government in 2013. The initiative aims to promote economic cooperation and connectivity between countries in Asia, Europe, and Africa along the ancient Silk Road trade routes. It encompasses a vast network of infrastructure projects, such as ports, roads, railroads, and power plants, as well as financial and policy support for participating countries.

The BRI is seen as a key component of China's global economic and strategic ambitions, and is expected to have a significant impact on the participating countries and the global economy as a whole. Supporters of the initiative argue that it will help to spur economic growth and development in participating countries, while critics raise concerns about issues such as debt sustainability, environmental impacts, and the potential for unequal benefits.

Despite these concerns, the BRI has gained broad support from participating countries, with more than 80 countries and international organisations signing on to participate in the initiative. The BRI has also been welcomed by the international community as a means of promoting economic cooperation and reducing tensions, and has been endorsed by organisations such as the United Nations and the World Bank. Overall, the BRI represents a major effort by China to shape the global economic landscape and assert its role as a major player on the world stage.

A. Objectives

The Belt and Road Initiative (BRI) is a development strategy and framework proposed by the Chinese government in 2013. The main objective of BRI is to build a trade and infrastructure network connecting Asia, Europe, and Africa along the ancient Silk Road trade routes. The initiative aims to enhance connectivity and collaboration between countries in these regions, thereby promoting economic growth, trade, and cultural exchange.

The BRI seeks to achieve several key objectives, including:

- Boosting economic growth: The initiative aims to boost economic growth in participating countries by increasing cross-border trade and investment.
- Enhancing connectivity: The BRI seeks to enhance connectivity between countries through the development of infrastructure such as ports, roads, railways, and airports. This is expected to improve access to markets, reduce transportation costs, and increase economic cooperation.
- Promoting regional integration: The BRI seeks to promote regional integration by encouraging countries to work together to address common challenges and pursue shared opportunities.
- Strengthening cultural ties: The initiative aims to strengthen cultural ties between countries by promoting cultural exchanges and exchanges of expertise.
- Supporting sustainable development: The BRI seeks to support sustainable development by promoting environmentally friendly and socially responsible development projects.
- Overall, the BRI is designed to promote economic growth, enhance connectivity, and strengthen cooperation among countries in the regions it encompasses.

B. Background

The Belt and Road Initiative (BRI), also known as One Belt One Road (OBOR) or the Silk Road Economic Belt and the 21st Century Maritime Silk Road, is a global development strategy proposed by the Chinese government in 2013. It aims to promote economic cooperation and development through infrastructure construction and investment in countries along the ancient Silk Road trade routes, which connected China with Europe and other parts of Asia. The initiative encompasses both land-based economic corridors and maritime routes, and is intended to increase connectivity, stimulate economic growth, and enhance trade and investment between participating countries.

The BRI has been widely seen as China's most ambitious foreign policy initiative, with a focus on infrastructure projects, such as highways, ports, power plants, and other facilities in countries along the routes. The initiative has garnered support from many countries, but has also faced criticism from some quarters, who have raised concerns about the environmental and social impacts of the projects, as well as the potential geopolitical implications of increased Chinese influence in participating countries.

Project name

The Belt and Road Initiative (BRI), also known as the One Belt One Road (OBOR) strategy, is a development strategy and framework, proposed by the Chinese government, to enhance economic cooperation and development through infrastructure projects along the ancient Silk Road trade routes that connect Asia, Europe, and Africa. The official name for the initiative is the Silk Road Economic Belt and 21st-Century Maritime Silk Road Development Strategy, which was initially abbreviated as the OBOR. However, since 2016, the Chinese government has changed the English translation to the Belt and Road Initiative to emphasize that it is an inclusive development initiative rather than a strategy.

International relations

The Belt and Road Initiative has been a topic of much discussion and analysis in the realm of international relations. Some believe it to be a way for China to extend its economic and political influence, while others see it as a means of improving connectivity and promoting trade between different regions. Regardless of the motivations behind it, the Belt and Road Initiative has already had a significant impact on countries along its proposed route, with China investing billions of dollars in infrastructure projects to improve basic facilities.

In South Asia, for example, China has invested heavily in countries like Pakistan, Nepal, Sri Lanka, Bangladesh, and Afghanistan, which has not only boosted the local economy but also enhanced

China's military and trade presence in the region. Furthermore, China's engagement in the Caucasus region, through its cooperation with Armenia, highlights the potential for the Belt and Road Initiative to serve as a new economic corridor connecting different regions.

In India, China has emerged as a rapidly growing source of Foreign Direct Investment (FDI), jumping from the 28th rank in 2014 to the 17th largest in 2016. This highlights the potential for China to deepen its economic ties with other countries through the Belt and Road Initiative.

Western regions

The Belt and Road Initiative aims to link China with Europe and other regions along the ancient Silk Road trade routes, including the western regions. The western regions refer to areas such as Central Asia, the Caucasus, and the Middle East. China's efforts to improve connectivity in the western regions include investments in infrastructure projects such as roads, bridges, ports, and pipelines. The initiative also aims to increase trade and investment between China and countries in the western regions, and to promote economic development in these areas. The western regions are seen as strategically important for China due to their proximity to the energy-rich countries of the Middle East, as well as their position as a crossroads between Europe, Asia, and Africa. By improving infrastructure and economic ties in the western regions, China hopes to increase its influence in the region and promote stability and growth in these countries.

Leadership

The Belt and Road Initiative (BRI) has a steering committee that was established in late 2014 and was publicly announced in February 2015. The committee, which reports directly to the State Council of China, is made up of several important political figures and is seen as evidence of the initiative's importance to the Chinese government. The former Vice-Premier, Zhang Gaoli, was named as the leader of the group, with Wang Huning, Wang Yang, Yang Jing, and Yang Jiechi serving as deputy leaders.

In March 2015, the principles, framework, and key areas of cooperation for the initiative were outlined by China's State Council. The BRI is considered a key component of China's foreign policy and was incorporated into its constitution in 2017.

For BRI projects in African countries, the Forum on China-Africa Cooperation (FOCAC) serves as a major multilateral cooperation mechanism. Similarly, the China-Arab States Cooperation Forum (CASCF) coordinates BRI projects in Arab states.

Financing

The Asian Infrastructure Investment Bank (AIIB) was established in 2015 as a development bank focused on financing infrastructure projects. It was created with the aim of addressing the growing infrastructure needs in Asia, promoting regional integration, driving economic development and improving access to social services. The legal framework of AIIB is governed by the Articles of Agreement signed in Beijing in 2015. The bank has a total authorized capital of $100 billion, with 75% of the funding coming from Asia and Oceania. China is the largest stakeholder with 26.63% of voting rights. The board of governors serves as the highest decision-making body of the bank, which started its operations on January 16, 2016 and approved its first set of loans in June of the same year.

Silk Road Fund

The Silk Road Fund was established in November 2014, announced by Chinese Communist Party leader Xi Jinping. It is a $40 billion investment fund separate from traditional banks and not related to the China-Pakistan Economic Corridor (CPEC) investment. The fund invests in businesses rather than lending money for projects. The first project the fund invested in was the Karot Hydropower Project in Pakistan, with the Chinese government promising to provide at least $350 million by 2030 to finance it. Work on the project started in January 2016 by the Sanxia Construction Corporation.

Debt sustainability

In 2017, China joined the G20 guidelines for sustainable financing and in 2019, it joined the G20 principles for quality infrastructure investment. The World Bank's chief economist, Carmen Reinhart, stated that 60% of the lending from Chinese banks goes to developing countries, where the loans are negotiated bilaterally and kept secret. Despite this, there is no evidence to support the claims that China is using debt trap diplomacy. However, there are concerns regarding the ability of Chinese banks to control risks, as they do not have a good record of efficiently allocating resources. The COVID-19 pandemic has affected some BRI projects and has led to a slump in demand for commodities in debtor countries, leading to possible debt defaults. In response to the pandemic, the Group of 20 agreed to freeze debt payments for struggling countries, but interest on Chinese loans continued to accrue. In 2020, Chinese leader Xi Jinping decided to cancel interest-free loans for some African countries, which has been a controversial topic in China due to its own poverty-stricken areas.

C. Infrastructure networks

The Belt and Road Initiative (BRI) is a major infrastructure development effort aimed at enhancing connectivity between 60 countries, primarily in Asia and Europe but also including Oceania and East Africa. The cost of the initiative is estimated to be between $4-8 trillion and is being supported by the Silk Road Fund and the Asian Infrastructure Investment Bank, while being technically coordinated by the B&R Summit Forum. The initiative involves the construction of land corridors, including the New Eurasian Land Bridge, which connects Western China to Western Russia through Kazakhstan and the Silk Road Railway, and the China-Pakistan Economic Corridor, which is a collection of infrastructure projects in Pakistan aimed at modernizing the country's transportation and energy infrastructure. The focus of the BRI is to improve connectivity, as China's economic growth has been largely supported by exports and the import of raw materials. China has already built cross-border highways and expressway networks to nearly every nearby region and has seen a surge in rail usage after the COVID-19 pandemic congested air freight and sea shipping.

Silk Road Economic Belt

In 2013, China's President Xi Jinping proposed the establishment of a new economic area known as the Silk Road Economic Belt (SREB) during his visits to Astana, Kazakhstan, and Southeast Asia. The SREB initiative aims to increase cultural exchanges and trade by building hard and soft infrastructure, such as roads and rail links, as well as trade agreements and a shared legal structure with a court system. The initiative covers countries along the original Silk Road, as well as South Asia and Southeast Asia. The proposed SREB is divided into three belts - the North Belt passing through Central Asia and Russia to Europe, the Central Belt going through Central Asia and West Asia to the Persian Gulf and Mediterranean, and the South Belt extending from China through Southeast Asia, South Asia, and to the Indian Ocean through Pakistan. Additionally, the SREB will integrate China with Central Asia through Kazakhstan's Nurly Zhol infrastructure program, and many of the countries in the belt are members of the China-led Asian Infrastructure Investment Bank (AIIB).

21st Century Maritime Silk Road

The "21st Century Maritime Silk Road" is an initiative aimed at investing and promoting collaboration among countries in Southeast Asia, Oceania, and Africa. The Maritime Silk Road is a sea route that starts from the Chinese coast, passes through several countries in Southeast Asia, the South Pacific Ocean, and the Indian Ocean, and reaches to Africa. Most of the countries along this route are also members of the Asian Infrastructure Investment Bank. The primary objective of the

Maritime Silk Road is to increase trade and cultural exchanges between these countries. The maritime route is considered more attractive for trade due to the larger number of states and markets along the way, as well as the higher population numbers. Africa is considered an important market, raw material supplier, and platform for China's Silk Road expansion initiatives, with several ports and infrastructure projects being built along the coast of the continent.

The Chinese Silk Road strategy includes investing in large areas of Africa for the construction and operation of transportation infrastructure such as train routes, roads, airports, and industry. Additionally, China is participating in the construction of buildings and dams in various African countries. In Europe, China is focusing its investments in the port of Piraeus and other European ports such as Sines in Portugal and Adriatic logistics hub around Trieste, Italy. The international free zone of Trieste provides special areas for storage, handling, processing, and transit of goods. The direct train connections between China and Europe, such as from Chengdu to Vienna, are partially stagnating or discontinued, but there are new weekly rail connections between Trieste and other European cities. Intra-European infrastructure projects aim to adapt trade flows to current needs, such as the expansion of the Belgrade-Budapest railway line and the construction of a high-speed train between Milan, Venice, and Trieste. The maritime Silk Road connects Poland, the Baltic States, Northern Europe, and Central Europe to the Adriatic ports and Piraeus to East Africa, India, and China. The maritime route via Trieste reduces transport costs between Asia and Europe and has ecological advantages with lower CO_2 emissions. The Brenner Base Tunnel, which will link the upper Adriatic with southern Germany, makes the port of Trieste a special target for Chinese investments, including agreements with the China Communications Construction Company (CCCC) to promote the ports of Trieste and Genoa, and investment from other entities such as the Hamburg port logistics group HHLA and Duisburger Hafen AG. There are also numerous collaborations in the Upper Adriatic region.

Ice Silk Road

Representatives from Vnesheconombank stated that Russia and China are engaging in discussions about the construction of the Ice Silk Road along the Northern Sea Route in the Arctic. The shipping route will be within Russian territorial waters. China COSCO Shipping Corp. has already completed several trial trips on the Arctic shipping routes and companies from both countries are working together on oil and gas exploration and other infrastructure, tourism and scientific projects. The conference, Development of the Shelf of Russia and CIS, had representatives from the leadership of Russian corporations and foreign auditors and consulting centers, including Gazprom, Lukoil, Rosatom, Rosgeologiya, Vnesheconombank, Morneftegazproekt, Murmanshelf, Russian Helicopters, Deloitte, and Norwegian Rystad Energy, among others.

Super grid

The super grid project aims to develop six ultra high voltage electrical grids across China, Northeast Asia, Southeast Asia, South Asia, Central Asia and West Asia. The wind power resources of Central Asia would form one component of this grid

Additionally proposed

The Bangladesh-China-India-Myanmar Economic Corridor was suggested to connect southern China with Myanmar and was initially considered as part of the Belt and Road Initiative. However, since the second Belt and Road Forum in 2019, it has been removed from the list of projects due to India's refusal to participate in the Belt and Road Initiative.

Projects

The Belt and Road Initiative has involved 149 countries and 30 international organizations. Infrastructure projects include transportation, energy, and communication developments. Major projects include the China-Pakistan Economic Corridor and railway projects in Laos and Khorgas.

Here is the investment by country in billion dollars from 2014 to 2018:

Country	Construction Investment (in billion $)
Pakistan	31.9
Nigeria	23.2
Bangladesh	17.5
Malaysia	15.8
Indonesia	16.8
Egypt	15.3
UAE	14.7
Singapore	24.3
Malaysia	14.1
Russian Federation	10.4
South korea	8.1
Israel	7.9

D.Ecological issues

The Belt and Road Initiative (BRI) has raised concerns among environmental organizations. A report by the World Wide Fund for Nature and HSBC highlighted the risks and opportunities posed by the BRI for sustainable development, including overuse of resources, ecosystem disruption, and pollution. The construction of coal-fired power plants as part of the BRI is contributing to greenhouse gas emissions and global warming. Environmental problems in Central Asian nations, such as glacier melting, species preservation, desertification, soil erosion, mining practices, and water and air pollution, have also been cited.

Critics have also raised the issue of "pollution outsourcing" to poorer countries, where governments may ignore environmental consequences. The presence of Chinese coal-powered plants in Serbia has increased the country's reliance on coal and resulted in air and soil pollution. Chinese energy companies are expected to account for nearly half of the new coal plants to be built in the next decade.

The development of port infrastructure and shipping associated with the BRI's maritime component may also have an impact on marine habitats and species. However, Chinese leader Xi Jinping has stated that the BRI should be "green, low-carbon, circular, and sustainable" in accordance with the 2030 Agenda for Sustainable Development. A report by the United Nations Development Programme and CCIEE view the BRI as an opportunity for environmental protection if used to promote green trade, finance, and investment.

The Belt and Road Initiative International Green Development Coalition (BRIGC) was launched to integrate sustainable development into the BRI's priorities. However, it remains to be seen whether the best practices outlined by the coalition will be implemented. Environmental protection goals are only outlined in informal guidelines, and member nations may prioritize economic development over environmental protections, potentially leading to neglect of environmental policy.

In September 2021, Xi Jinping announced that China will "step up support" for developing countries to adopt green and low-carbon energy and will no longer finance overseas coal-fired power plants.

Human rights accusations

The American NGO China Labor Watch has reported on the numerous human rights violations inflicted upon Chinese migrant workers sent abroad. Allegations abound of companies confiscating passports on arrival, protecting illegal business visas, threatening repercussions for refusing to comply with demands, inadequate medical care and rest, restriction of personal liberty and freedom of speech, forcing workers to do overtime, cancelling holidays, delaying wages, false advertising and broken promises, intimidating workers with high fines if they try to leave, providing inadequate living and working conditions, and punishing those who lead protests.

E.Reactions and criticism

Support

On 4 February 2022, Russian President Vladimir Putin and Chinese leader Xi Jinping met, during which they discussed the strategic partnership between their countries. This partnership was reinforced when Polish President Andrzej Duda and Xi Jinping signed a declaration of such in June 2016. Overall, more than 130 countries have endorsed the Belt and Road Initiative, with Russia and China having 150 common projects including natural gas pipelines and the Polar Silk Road. Singapore has also endorsed the BRI and invested heavily in related projects to gain global relevance and to strengthen their economic ties with BRI recipients.

The Philippines, led by President Rodrigo Duterte, adjusted its policy to favor Chinese claims in the South China Sea. Yanis Varoufakis, the former Greek Minister of Finance, wrote positively of the Belt and Road Initiative and its ability to combine a sense of self-interest with a genuine commitment to negotiate. China engaged in partnerships with 18 Arab countries, called "Build the Belt and Road, Share Development and Prosperity". Eastern European countries, Italy, and Malaysia have all pledged support for the BRI, with the latter's former Prime Minister Mahathir Mohamad stating that it can bring land-locked countries of Central Asia closer to the sea and grow in wealth.

Russian political scientist Sergey Karaganov, who is considered close to Russian President Vladimir Putin, has advocated for a united Sino-Russian strategy to unify a Eurasian bloc. He argues that the Eurasian Economic Union (EEU) and China's Belt and Road Initiative, will work together to promote economic integration throughout the region.

Opposition

In response to the Belt and Road Initiative (BRI), the United States, Japan, and Australia formed the Blue Dot Network in 2019, followed by the G7's Build Back Better World initiative in 2021. The US also proposed the Free and Open Indo-Pacific strategy (FOIP), which includes three pillars – security, economics, and governance. India has expressed objections to the BRI, particularly the China–Pakistan Economic Corridor (CPEC), due to its perceived infringement on their sovereignty and territorial integrity. Former Malaysian Prime Minister Mahathir Mohamad initially advised countries against joining the BRI, but his opinion has since changed.

Despite strong historical tensions between Vietnam and China, the former has yet to decide whether to support or oppose the Belt and Road Initiative (BRI). South Korea, on the other hand, has sought to develop its own vision for an east-west connection, the Eurasia Initiative (EAI), which aims to stimulate economic, political, and social activity from Europe through the Korean Peninsula. Additionally, President Moon Jae-in has proposed the New Southern Policy (NSP) in order to strengthen ties with Southeast Asia.

In Europe, while countries such as Italy and Greece have joined the BRI, others have expressed a more ambivalent stance. German Chancellor Angela Merkel has called for a reciprocal relationship between the two sides, while French President Emmanuel Macron has stated that the ancient Silk Roads were never solely Chinese. In response, the European Commission Chief Jean-Claude Juncker and Japanese Prime Minister Shinzo Abe signed an infrastructure agreement to coordinate infrastructure, transport and digital projects in order to counter China's Belt and Road Initiative.

In 2018, the Australian state of Victoria's premier, Daniel Andrews, signed a Memorandum of Understanding (MOU) with China as part of the Belt and Road Initiative (BRI) to increase infrastructure ties and relations. However, the federal government was not supportive of the decision, with Home Affairs Minister Peter Dutton describing it as "a propaganda initiative" and Prime Minister Scott Morrison stressing the need for states to respect federal government policy. In April 2021, Foreign Minister Marise Payne announced Australia's withdrawal from the BRI, with the federal government's stance reflecting the deteriorating relations between Australia and China due to China's alleged attempts at economic coercion in response to Australia's support for an investigation into the origins of COVID-19, as well as Australia's backing of the US against China in regional disputes such as the issue of Taiwan and the South China Sea.

F.Accusations of neo-imperialism and debt-trap diplomacy

Accusations

There has been widespread concern that the Belt and Road Initiative (BRI) could be a form of neo-colonialism due to China's alleged practice of debt-trap diplomacy to finance infrastructure projects. Proponents of the BRI, however, argue that it has provided a platform for increased market access, improved resource prices, improved infrastructure, created employment and spurred industrialization and technology transfer in host countries. This has been contested by Tanzanian President John Magufuli, who called the loan agreements for BRI projects in his country "exploitative and awkward." He suggested that Chinese financiers had set "tough conditions," such as a 33-year guarantee and a 99-year lease on a port construction, which he thought could only be accepted by "mad people." Magufuli also noted Chinese contractors wanted to take the land as their own, but his government had to compensate them for drilling the project construction.

Chinese sovereignty slicing continues to be an increasingly concerning area of international economics, with S. K. Chatterji citing Tajikistan as an example of a nation that has been pressured to handover territory in exchange for debt repayment. Furthermore, President Félix Tshisekedi of the Democratic Republic of the Congo has called for the review of certain mining contracts signed with China by his predecessor. Additionally, China's plans to link Xinjiang province with Pakistan's Balochistan province via the Gwadar Port have met resistance from local fishermen who are protesting Chinese trawlers and illegal fishing.

Rebuttals

Debt-trap diplomacy, a theory suggesting that China is using its lending practices to trap developing countries in debt, has been criticized by scholars as a "meme" with no evidence to support it. Professor Deborah Bräutigam of the School of Advanced International Studies at Johns Hopkins University says that the media is promoting a wrong narrative that misrepresents the relationship between China and the countries it deals with, and the majority of debtor countries voluntarily signed the loans and have had positive experiences working with China. Anastasia Papadimitriou, a New York-based economist, explains that partnering countries are equally responsible in making deals with China and the Belt and Road Initiative is economic regionalism rather than neocolonialism. The Royal Institute of International Affairs in London confirms this, saying that the debt crisis in Sri Lanka was not caused by Chinese lending, but rather by the misconduct of local elites and Western-dominated financial markets. The Rhodium Group, an American research company, also analyzed Chinese debt renegotiations and found that China's leverage is often exaggerated and realistically limited.

Senior lecturer Darren Lim of the Australian National University and Professor Dawn C. Murphy of the U.S. Air War College both say that the "debt-trap diplomacy" claim is an exaggeration and misrepresentation. Political scientist Zhexin Zhang highlights the overwhelming enthusiasm of developing countries in the Belt and Road Initiative as evidence that invalidates the neo-colonialism argument. The Center for Global Development, a Washington-based think tank, found that between 2001 and 2017, China restructured or waived loan payments for 51 debtor nations without seizing state assets. Pradumna Bickram Rana and Jason Ji Xianbai of Nanyang Technological University in Singapore conclude that China's alleged debt-trap diplomacy is "more myth than reality" and that China has been willing to help these countries restructure their debt through forgiving policies.

Belt and Road educational community

The Belt and Road Initiative has five major goals, including people-to-people bonds. To promote this goal, China has allocated funds for scholarships for students and teachers along the Road and made efforts to attract and retain foreign talents. Xi'an Jiaotong University has established the University Alliance of the Silk Road to support the Belt and Road Initiative through research and academic exchange. In 2018, the France-China Foundation, a French think tank focused on the study of the New Silk Roads, was launched and is described as being supportive of the Belt and Road Initiative and China.

VII. CULTURAL AND IDEOLOGICAL DIFFERENCES:

Cultural and ideological differences refer to the distinctive beliefs, values, customs, behaviors, and institutions that exist among different groups of people. These differences can result from a variety of factors, including geography, history, language, religion, politics, and education. In the context of international relations, cultural and ideological differences can have a significant impact on the nature and outcome of interactions between countries. For example, differences in political systems, such as democracy and authoritarianism, can influence the type of relationship that two countries have with one another. Similarly, differences in cultural values, such as attitudes towards individual freedom and collective responsibility, can shape the way that countries perceive and respond to global challenges. Understanding and managing cultural and ideological differences is therefore an important aspect of building effective and sustainable relationships between nations.

IX. THE ROLE OF THE PRIVATE SECTOR:

The private sector refers to businesses and organizations that are owned and controlled by individuals, rather than by the government. The role of the private sector in an economy can vary widely depending on the country and its political and economic system. However, in general, the private sector is seen as playing a critical role in driving economic growth, creating jobs, and promoting innovation.

In many countries, the private sector is responsible for producing the majority of goods and services and for generating the majority of economic output. In these countries, the government often plays a supportive role, providing infrastructure, regulating markets, and creating policies that promote investment and growth.

In some countries, the private sector is also responsible for providing many essential social services, such as healthcare and education, which are traditionally the responsibility of the government. This can lead to a number of challenges, including issues around access and equity, but it can also create opportunities for increased innovation and efficiency in these sectors.

The role of the private sector in promoting sustainable development and addressing global challenges, such as climate change, is increasingly recognized. Many companies are taking proactive steps to reduce their carbon footprint, improve energy efficiency, and invest in renewable energy. Additionally, private sector investment in research and development can lead to the development of new technologies and approaches that can help address these challenges.

In conclusion, the role of the private sector in an economy is complex and multifaceted. However, it is widely recognized as playing a critical role in driving economic growth and promoting social and environmental progress

X. ANALYSIS AND CONCLUSION

In conclusion, the book could analyse the various themes and developments in modern Chinese history and their impact on China's rise as a global power. The book could examine China's rapid economic growth and its increasing global influence, its military modernization and involvement in multilateral institutions, its state-led capitalism and labor market, its innovation and political systems, and its profound social changes and regional tensions. The book could also consider the challenges and opportunities that China faces as it continues to rise as a global power and the implications for the international community. The book could then provide an overall conclusion on the factors that have contributed to China's rise as a global power and its prospects for the future.

A. Factors contributing to China's rise

The book could analyze the various factors that have contributed to China's rise as a global power, including its strong economic growth, military modernization, soft power initiatives, state-led capitalism, and focus on innovation. It could also examine the role that the country's political system has played in its development, as well as the social changes that have shaped its society and culture. The book could consider the challenges that China faces, such as regional tensions and the sustainability of its growth, and weigh their impact on its future prospects. Additionally, the book could examine the impact of China's rise on the international community and the implications for global politics and economics.

B. The impact of the rise of China on the world

The impact of China's rise as a global power has been significant and far-reaching. On one hand, China's economic growth has driven global economic growth and reduced poverty, particularly in the developing world. However, its growing military power and assertiveness in international affairs has led to increased tensions with other major powers, particularly the United States, and raised questions about the future of the international order. The Belt and Road Initiative has also had a major impact on global infrastructure and trade but has also been criticized for its lack of transparency and for imposing unsustainable debt levels on participating countries.

China's rise has also had a major impact on global politics and security. Its growing military power has led to increased concerns about regional stability and the balance of power in Asia, while its economic and political influence has had an impact on countries and regions around the world. China's growing role in international institutions, such as the United Nations and the World Trade

Organization, has also had a major impact on the functioning of these institutions and the way that global governance is conducted.

In conclusion, the rise of China as a global power has had a profound impact on the world, with both positive and negative effects. Understanding these effects and the factors that have contributed to China's rise is critical for understanding the future of the international order and the role that China will play in shaping it.

C. The future of China's role in the world

The book could delve into various scenarios for China's future role in the world, considering factors such as its economic growth, political stability, and military capabilities. It could explore how these factors may shape China's future relationships with other countries and its ability to project power and influence internationally. Additionally, the book could analyze the potential challenges that China may face in the coming years, such as environmental degradation, demographic changes, and rising global competition.

The book could also consider the implications of China's rise for the international community and its impact on the global economy and political system. This could include discussions of the potential for increased cooperation and competition with other major powers, and the impact on global governance and the international order. For instance, the book could analyze how China's rise as a global power may lead to shifts in the current balance of power, and how this may shape the future of international relations and global affairs.

Ultimately, the book could provide a comprehensive and nuanced analysis of China's rise as a global power and its future role in the world, considering the multiple factors and dynamics that are shaping its development and trajectory.